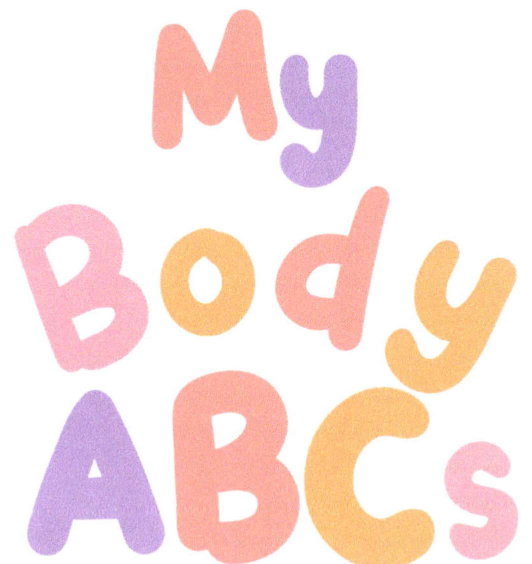

This book belongs to:

Written by Dr. Fei Zheng-Ward   Illustrated by Moch. Fajar Shobaru

Copyright © 2026 Fei Zheng-Ward

Identifiers: ISBN 979-8-89318-150-0 (eBook)
ISBN 979-8-89318-151-7 (paperback)
ISBN 979-8-89318-152-4 (hardcover)

A a

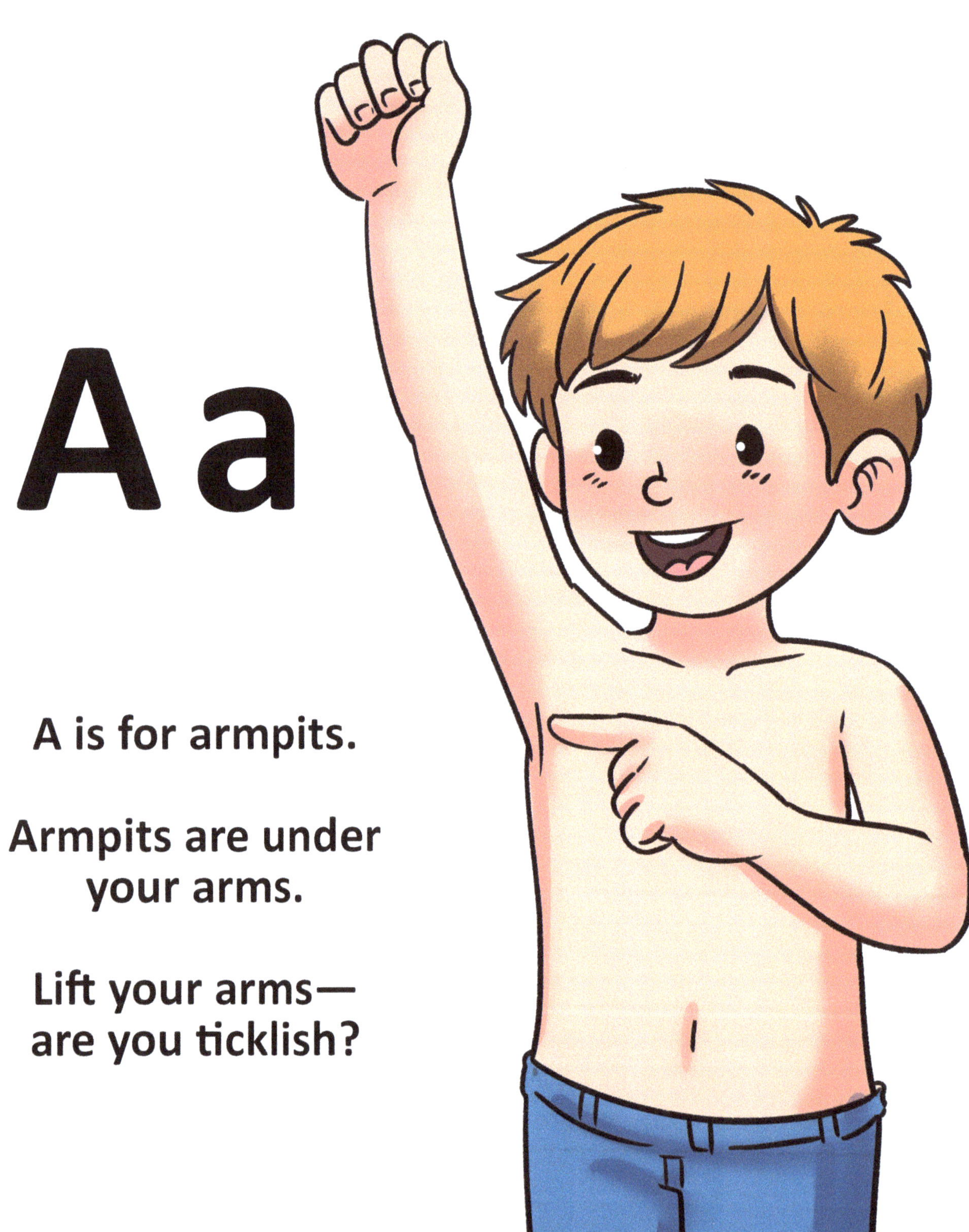

A is for armpits.

Armpits are under
your arms.

Lift your arms—
are you ticklish?

B b

B is for belly.

Did you know you can listen to a belly at work?

Your belly moves when you breathe.

Put your hand on your belly and take a slow breath.

Did you feel it move?

Cc

C is for cheeks.

D d

D is for diaphragm (DYE-uh-fram).

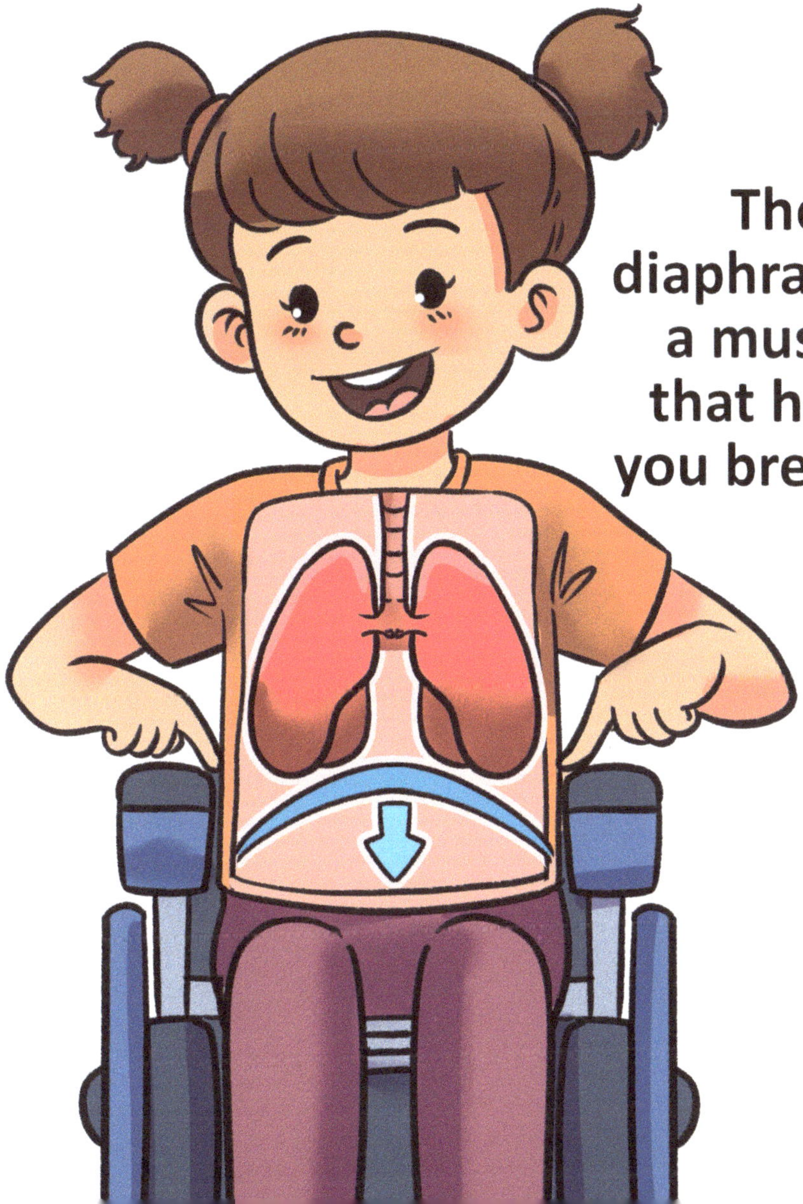

The diaphragm is a muscle that helps you breathe.

When you breathe out, your diaphragm moves up.

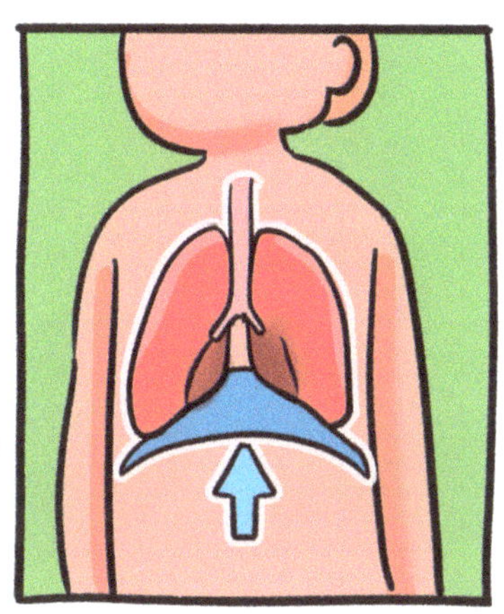

When you breathe in, your diaphragm moves down.

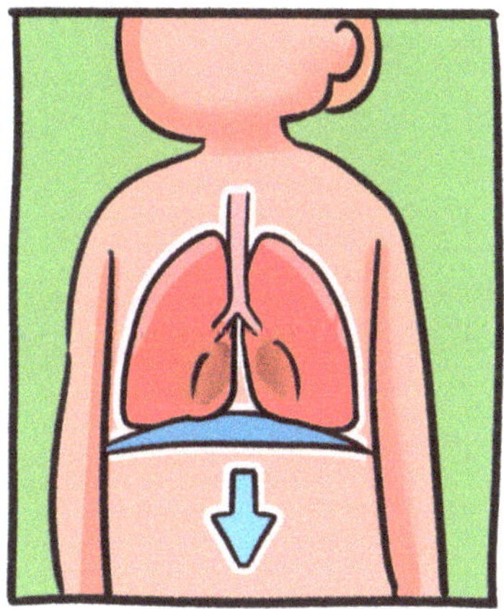

Eyelids protect your eyes.

Blink your eyes—open, close, open!

E e

E is for eyelids.

F f

F is for fingers.

Fingers help you touch and grab.

Trace the letters "F f" with your finger.

Gg

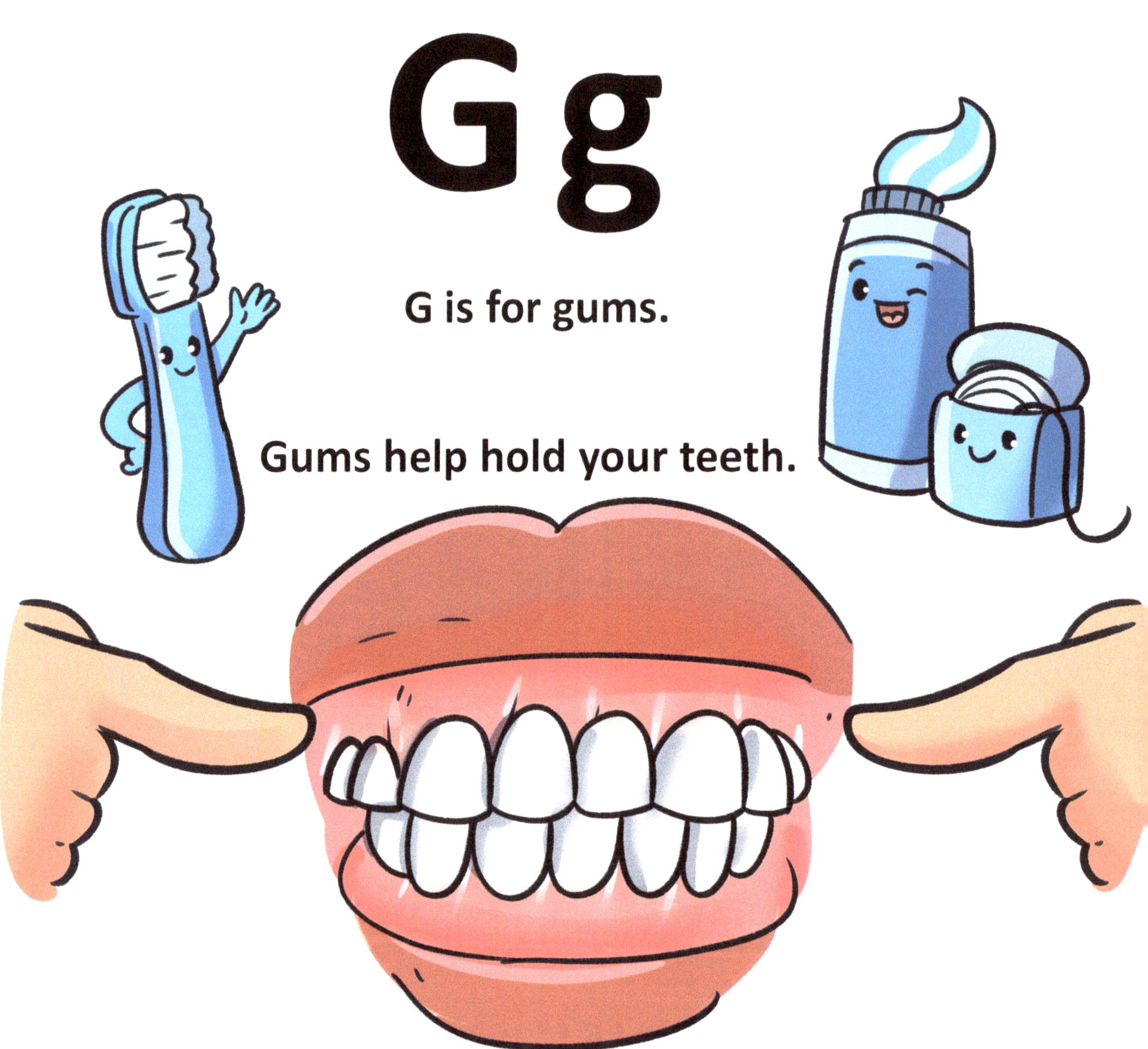

G is for gums.
Gums help hold your teeth.
Smile big and show your gums.

Hh

H is for head.

Your head helps you think.

What good ideas do you have?

I i

I is for iris.

The iris is the colorful part of your eye.

What color are your eyes?

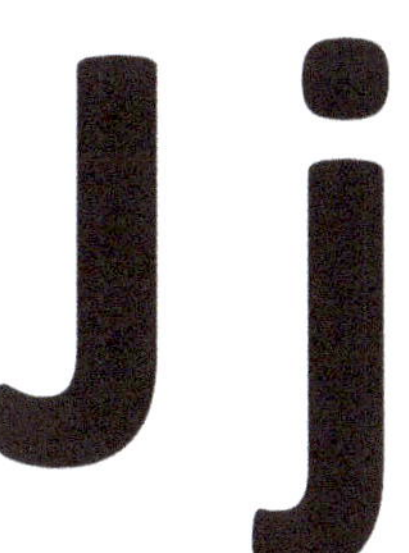

J is for jaw.

J j

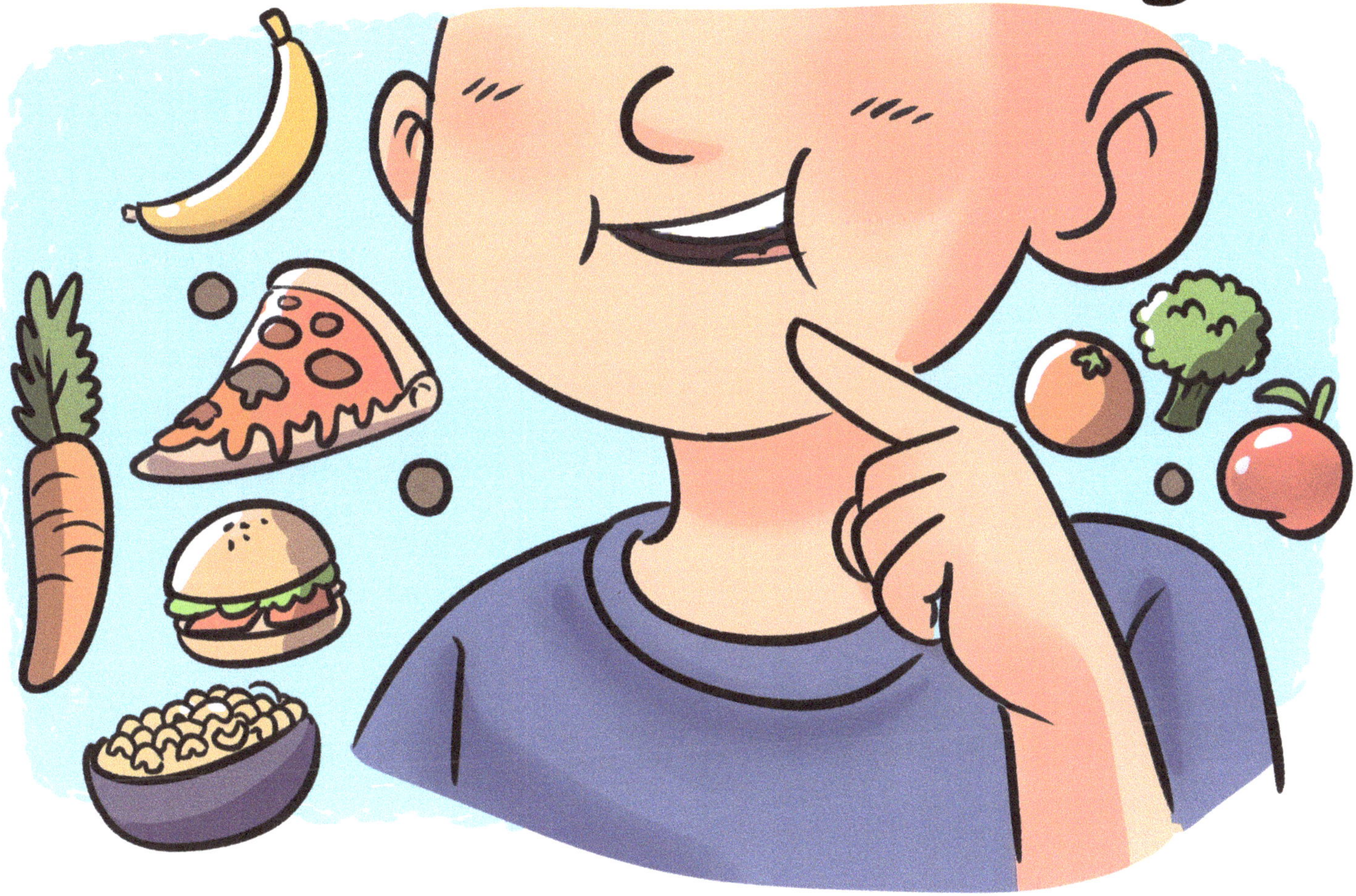

Your jaw helps you chew your favorite foods.

What are some of your favorites?

K k

K is for knees.

Knees bend when you move.

Bend your knees and do a little jump.

L is for lips.

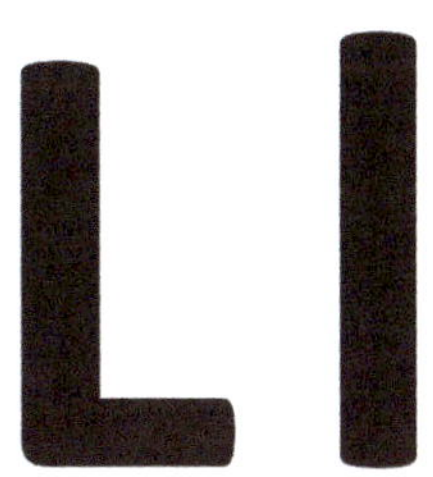

Lips help you talk and smile.
Blow a kiss with your lips!

M m

M is for muscles.

Muscles help you move and play.

Flex your muscles!

N is for nose.
Your nose helps you smell.
What is your favorite scent?
N n

O o

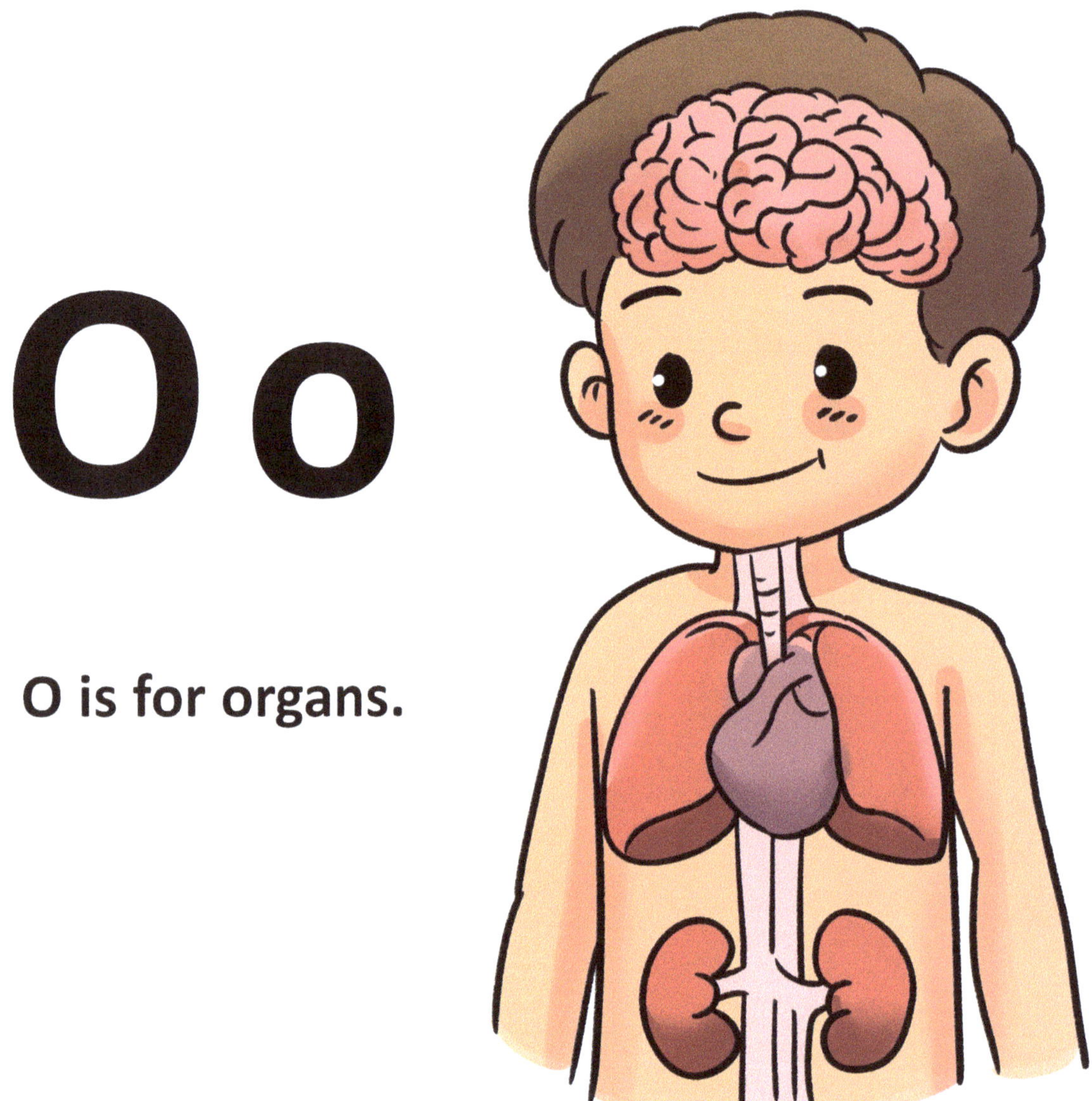

O is for organs.

**Organs help your body work.
Put your hand on your chest and feel your heart.**

P p

P is for phalanges (fuh-LAN-jeez).

Phalanges are the bones in your fingers and toes.

Wiggle your fingers and toes.

Q q

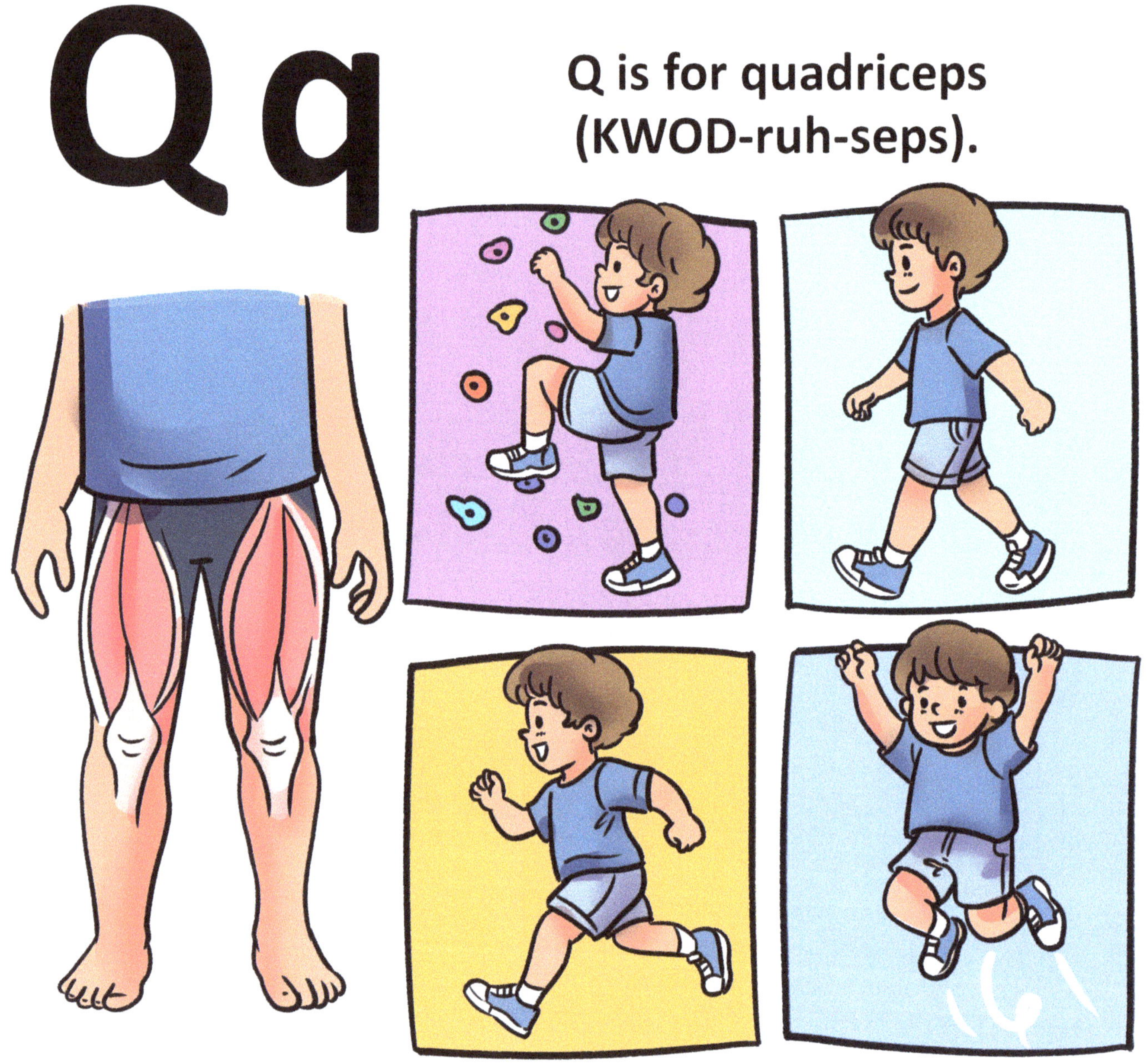

Quadriceps are big muscles in your legs.

Touch your legs and say, "Thank you, muscles!"

Rr

Ribs protect your
heart and lungs.

Gently touch the
sides of your chest to
feel your ribs.

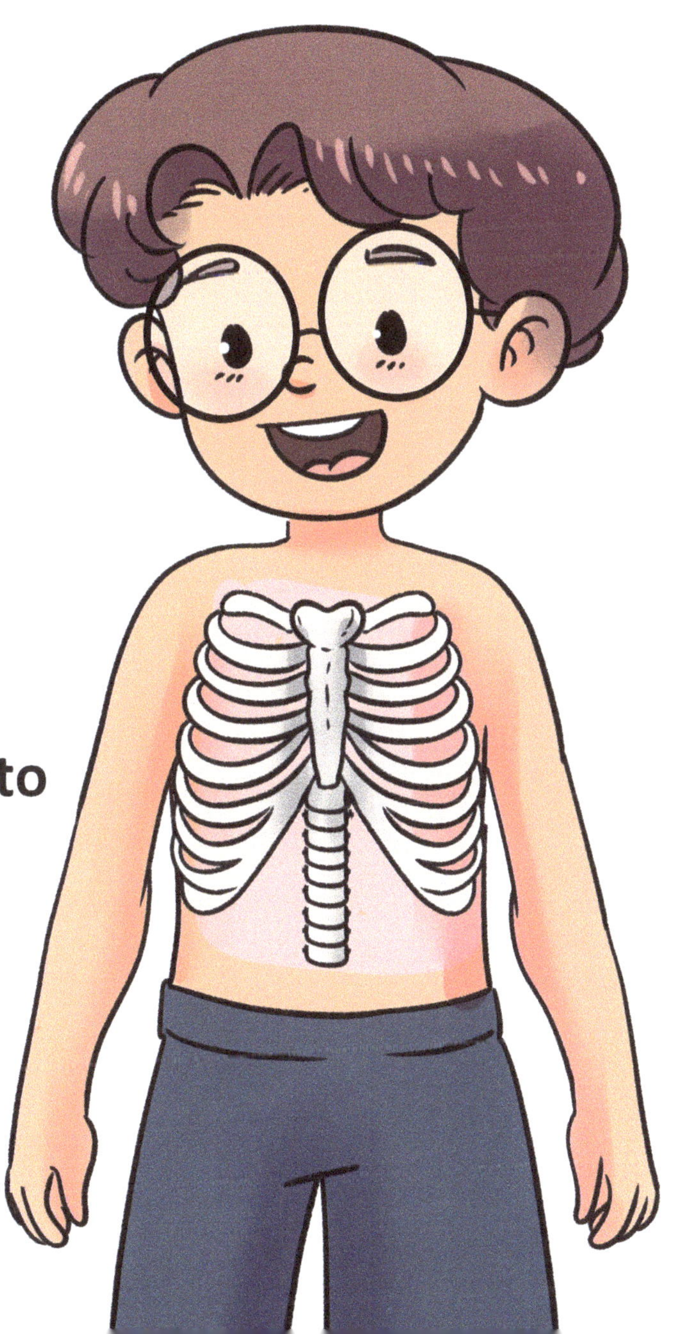

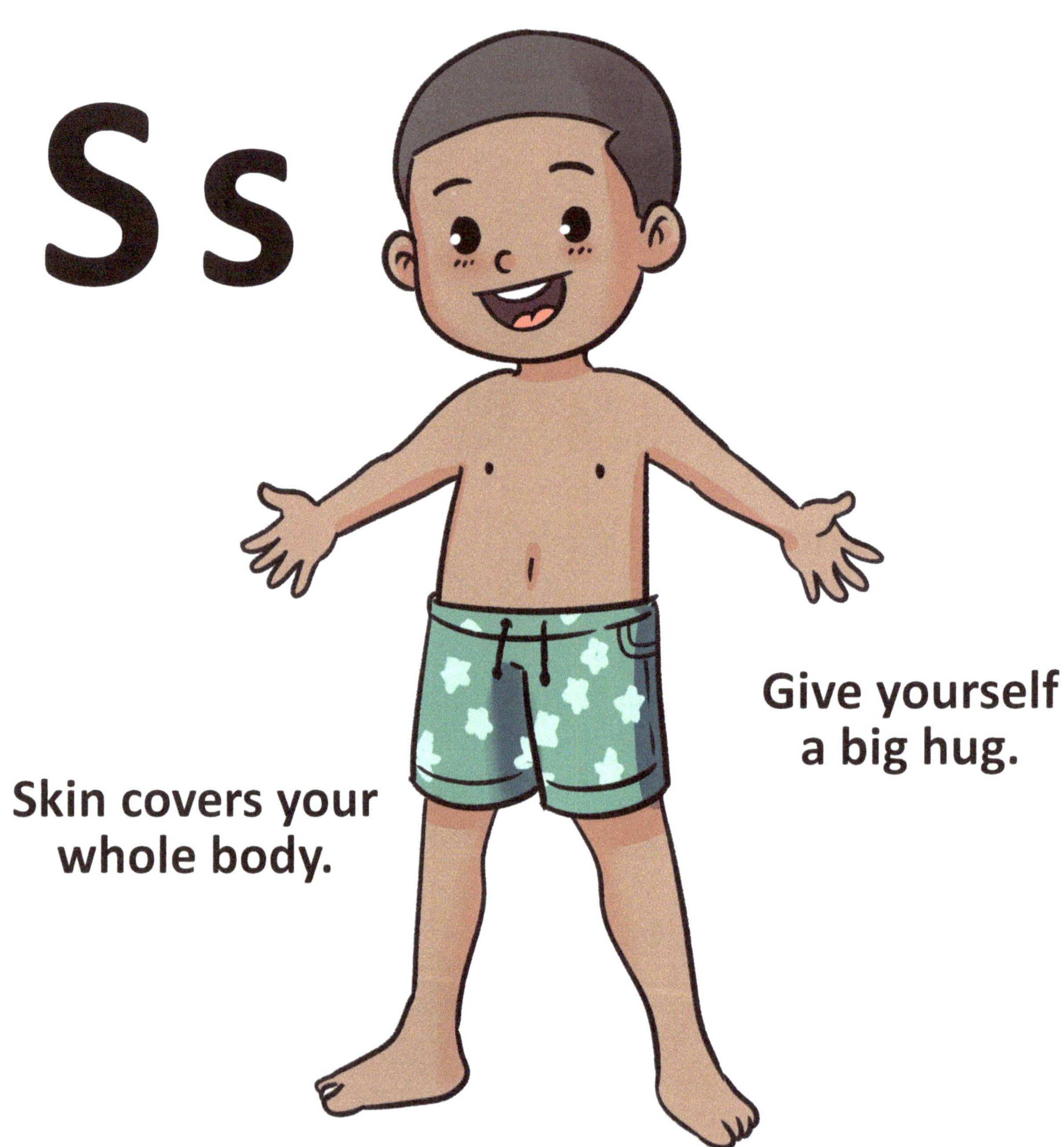

S is for skin.
Ss
Give yourself
a big hug.
Skin covers your
whole body.

T t

T is for tongue.

Your tongue helps you taste and talk.

Stick out your tongue and make a silly face.

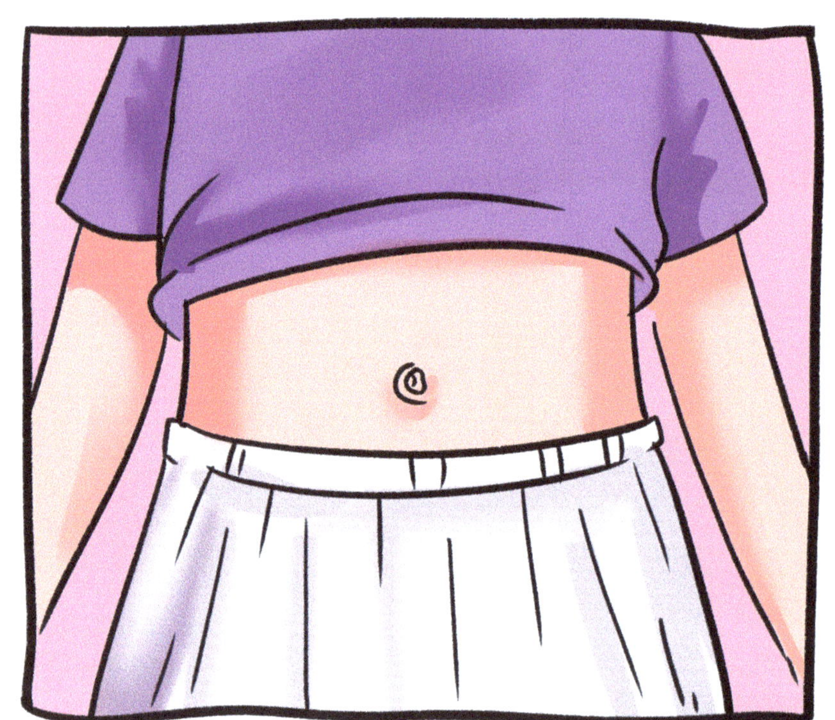

U u

U is for umbilicus (um-BIL-ih-kuhs).

Umbilicus means belly button.

Is yours an innie or an outie?

Both are great!

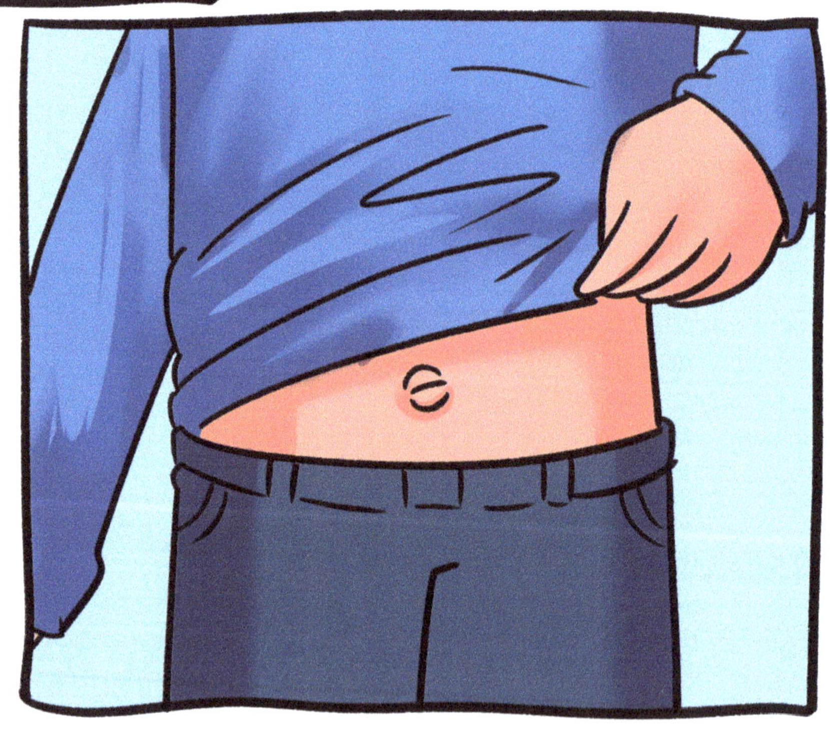

Vv

V is for vertebrae (VUR-tuh-bray).

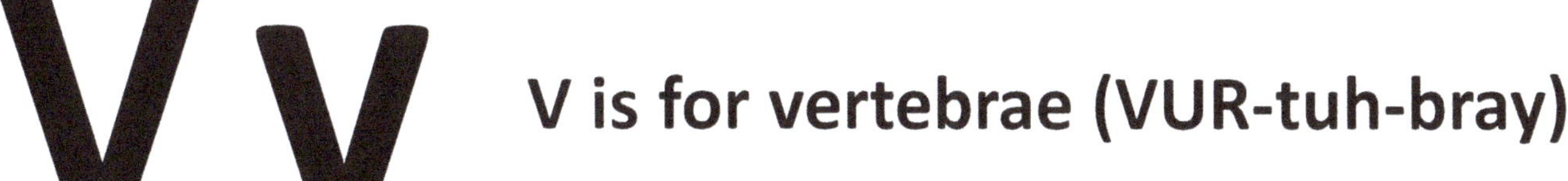

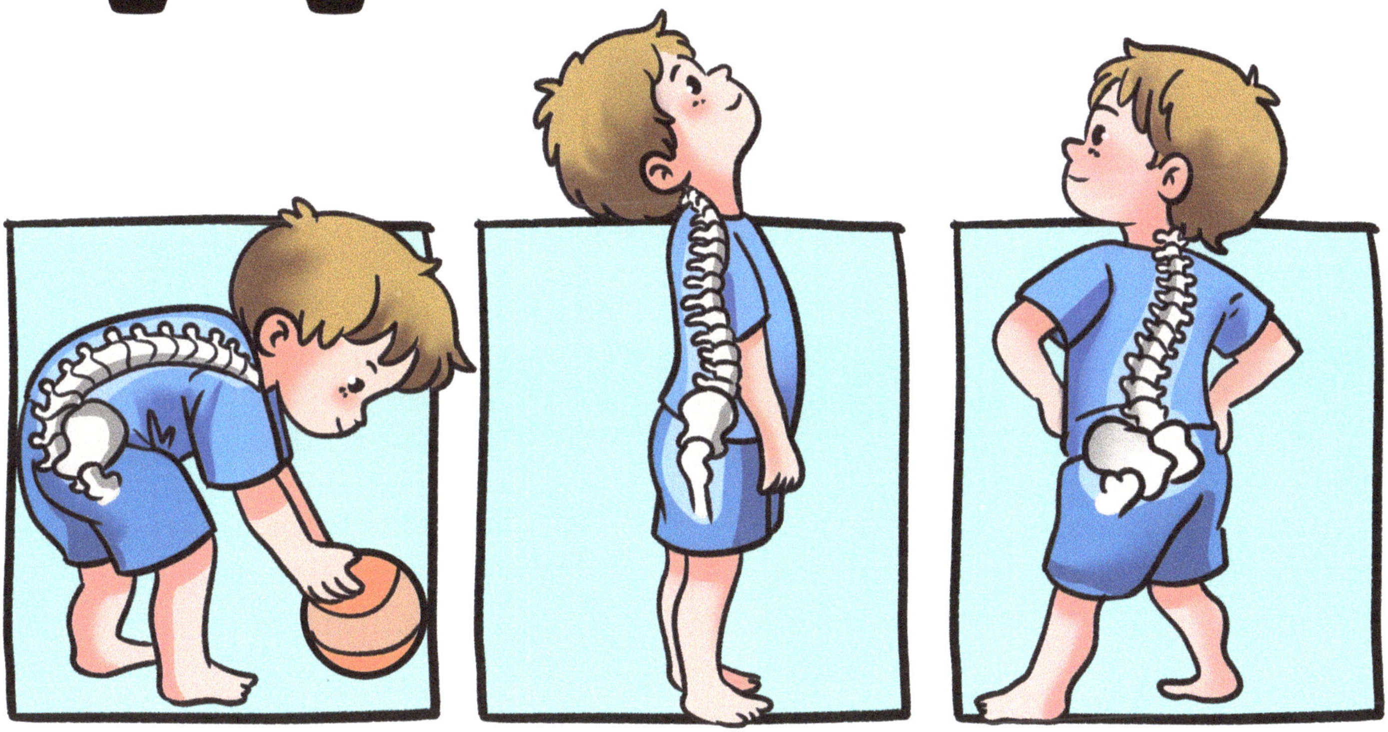

Vertebrae are the bones in your back.

Bend down, stretch tall, or bend side to side to move your vertebrae.

W w

W is for waist.

You bend at your waist.
Some people wear a belt around their waist.

X is for xiphoid (ZIGH-foyd).

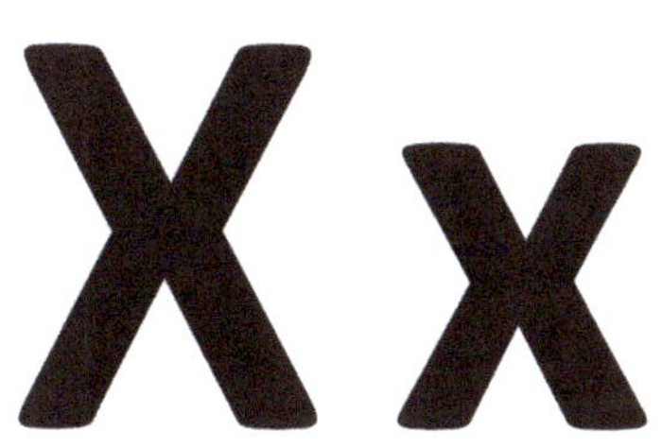

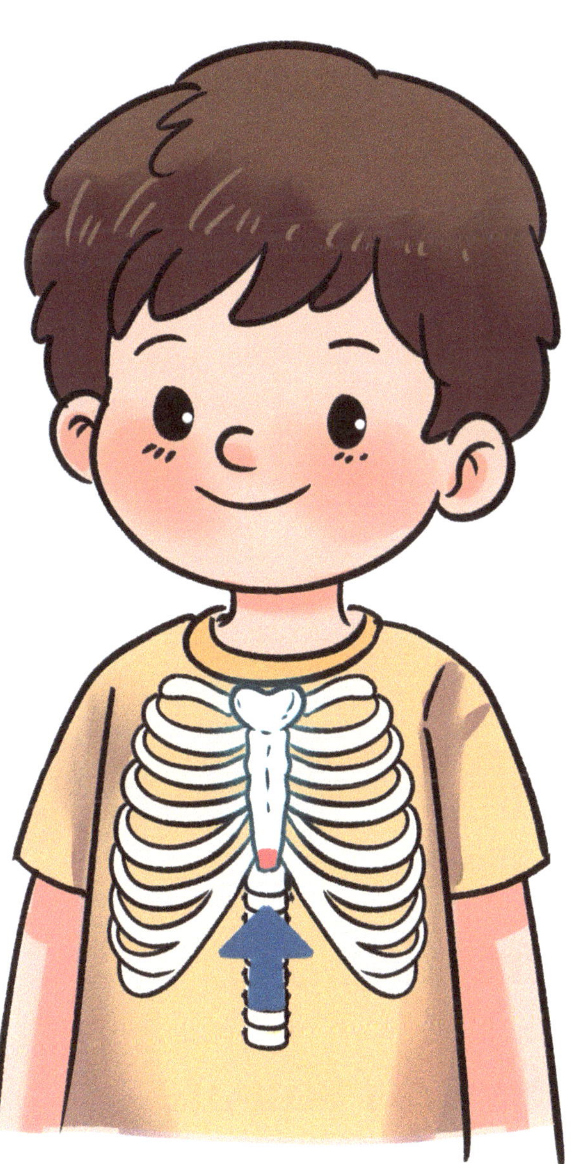

Xiphoid is a small part of your chest bone.

Can you find it with a gentle touch?

Yy

Y is for YOU.

YOU are amazing.

You are special the way you are.

Z is for zygomas (zy-GO-mas).

Zz

Zygomas are your cheekbones.

Touch your cheeks and give a big smile.

Books by the author

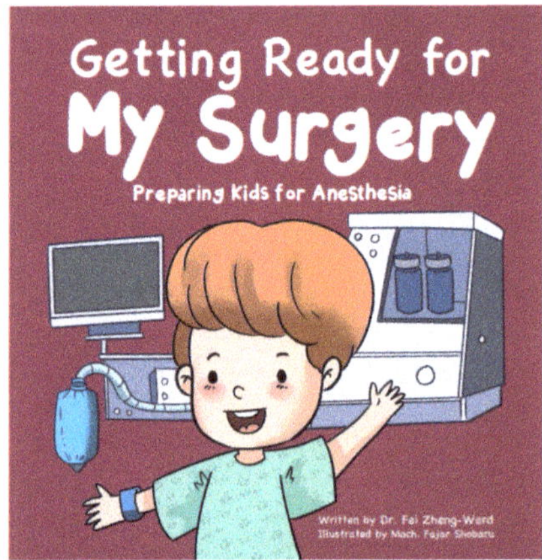

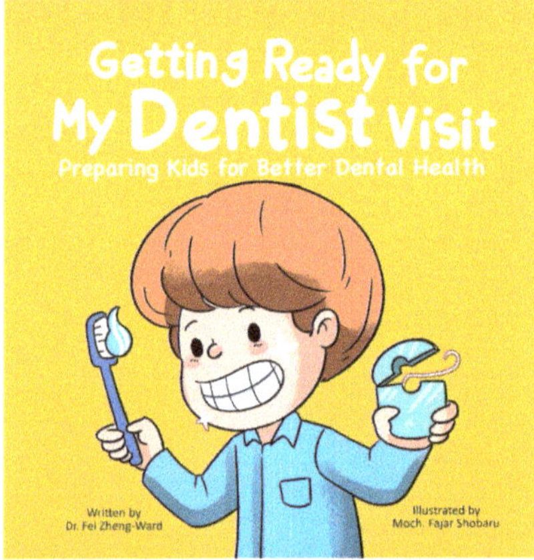

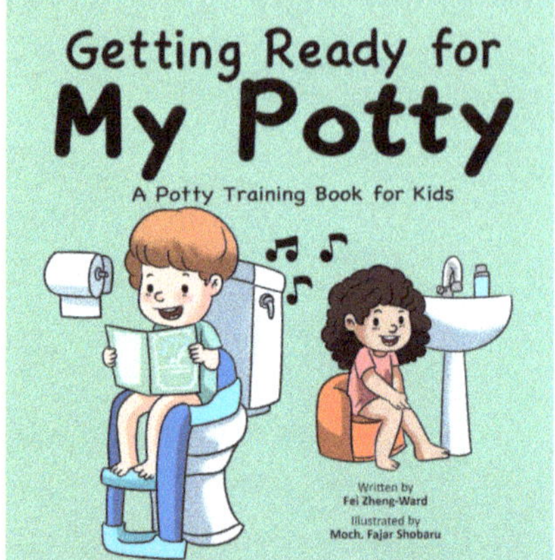

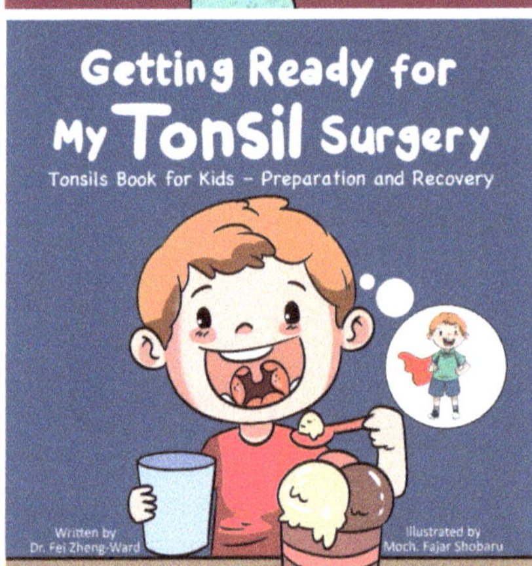

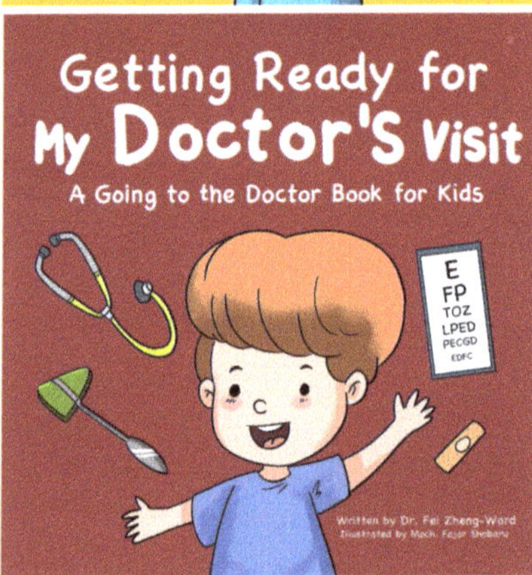

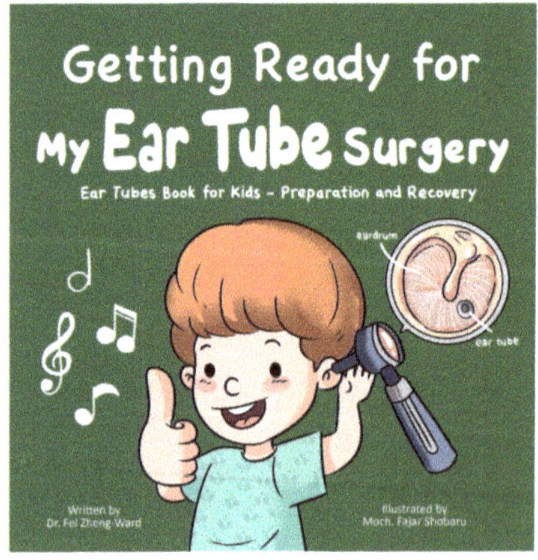

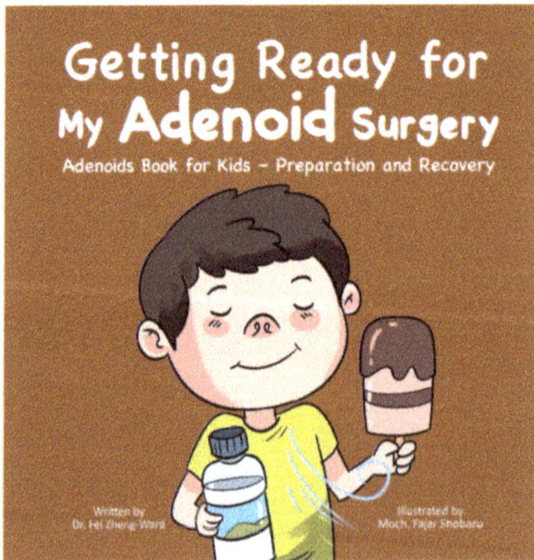

Forever and Always
By Your Side
Story by Fei Zheng-Ward
Illustrated by Nabila Amanda

Beautifully,
Uniquely
You
Story by Geoffrey Ward & Fei Zheng-Ward
Illustrated by Nabila Amanda

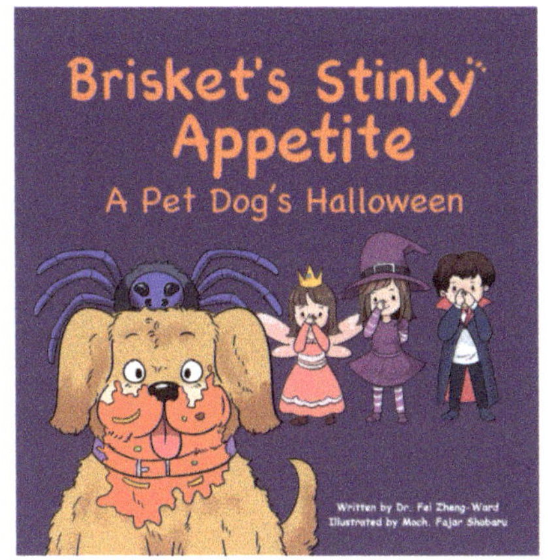

Brisket's Stinky Appetite
A Pet Dog's Halloween
Written by Dr. Fei Zheng-Ward
Illustrated by Mach. Fajar Shobaru

MEATBALL'S
ADVENTUROUS
APPETITE
A Pet Cat's Halloween
WRITTEN BY
DR. FEI ZHENG-WARD
ILLUSTRATED BY
ROKA STUDIO

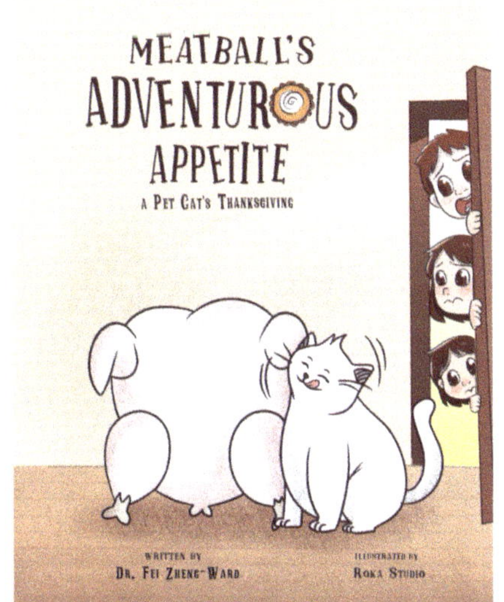

MEATBALL'S
ADVENTUROUS
APPETITE
A Pet Cat's Thanksgiving
WRITTEN BY
DR. FEI ZHENG-WARD
ILLUSTRATED BY
ROKA STUDIO

MEATBALL'S
ADVENTUROUS
APPETITE
A Pet Cat's Christmas Eve
WRITTEN BY
DR. FEI ZHENG-WARD
ILLUSTRATED BY
ROKA STUDIO

VICTORIA
SAVES THE DAY
A BOOK-READING GIRL
OUTSMARTS A WITCH
Story by Geoffrey Ward & Fei Zheng-Ward
Illustrated by Nabila Amanda

VICTORIA
SAVES THE DAY
A BRAVE GIRL SOLVES
A SCARY-MONSTER MYSTERY
Story by Fei Zheng-Ward & Geoffrey Ward
Illustrated by Nabila Amanda

VICTORIA
SAVES THE DAY
A CLEVER GIRL PLAYS TOOTH FAIRY
Story by Geoffrey Ward & Fei Zheng-Ward
Illustrated by Nabila Amanda